CM0074145?

SOUTH AFRICAN
TWO-FOOT
GAUGE

FEATURING THE LAST GARRATTS

Hugh Ballantyne

MP Middleton Press

Front Cover: NGG16 class Garratt no.110 is seen in the KwaZulu Natal countryside nearing Bomela with the 11.00 train from Port Shepstone to Harding on 13th August 1986. (Author)

Rear Cover: NG15 class 2-8-2 no.17 is coming up-grade in the Lang Kloof region with the 07.15 goods train from Assegaaibos to Avontuur on 24th June 1977. (Author)

Published May 2009
First reprint July 2013

ISBN 978 1 906008 51 2

© Middleton Press, 2009

Design Deborah Esher

Published by
> *Middleton Press*
> *Easebourne Lane*
> *Midhurst*
> *West Sussex*
> *GU29 9AZ*

Tel: 01730 813169
Fax: 01730 812601
Email: info@middletonpress.co.uk
www.middletonpress.co.uk

Printed in the United Kingdom by IJ Graphics, Guildford, Surrey. GU2 9XW

CONTENTS

INDEX

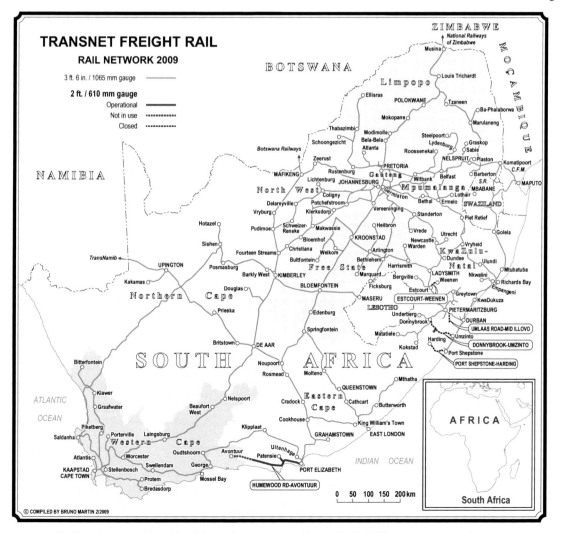

Rail network of South Africa showing location of 2 ft./610 mm gauge railways

INTRODUCTION

This album concerns the five two-foot gauge railways operated by South African Railways (SAR) in Natal and Eastern Cape Province to record their latter day operations until closure, and in some cases, present day limited working or partial preservation. It is also to commemorate the completion of the Welsh Highland Railway from Caernarvon to Porthmadog and that its mainstay locomotives are Garratts which had previously worked in South Africa. Very appropriately, it is also the centenary year in which the first Garratt type locomotive was built, in 1909, by Beyer Peacock of Manchester for the Tasmanian Government Railway.

It is not the intention to delve into the history of the five railways or locomotive details, but simply to portray some of the locations and traffic these railways operated. Each of the five lines, starting in the north and coming south down into the Eastern Cape, is briefly described. For much of their existence, the Natal lines were entirely Garratt worked (except in later years when the Alfred County Railway owned some NG15 2-8-2s and hired in two class 91 diesels), whereas the long two-foot gauge line in the Eastern Cape, also partially Garratt worked, used conventional locomotives and additionally, within the time span of this album, rigid framed class NG15 2-8-2s. These were cascaded down from South West Africa in1960, following the dieselisation of the railway in that arid region. The Avontuur railway also became a user of class 91 diesels in 1973.

With this in mind readers can enjoy the sight and sound of these attractive Garratts and NG15s now in the United Kingdom and, in reduced circumstances, on part of two of the railways in their native land described here; also on the new private railway at Sandstone, near Ficksberg in the Orange Free State.

THE GARRATT LOCOMOTIVE

This type of locomotive was the brainchild of Herbert William Garratt who was born in London on 8th June 1864. He served an apprenticeship from 1879 to 1882 in the locomotive works of the North London Railway at Bow. From here he went to Doxford's shipyard at Sunderland and spent time at sea as a third engineer until 1885 when he came back to railways as an inspector for some locomotives for the Central Argentine Railway. His time on the CAR gave him an insight to operating railways in difficult terrain. Other foreign posts were undertaken and in March 1902 he accepted a contract with the Lagos Government Railway to sort out the dire condition of that railway. Only three engines could move, and there was a lack of spares. By considerable effort he put the locomotive fleet back into working order and after only seven months the full train service was resumed. He then went to Peru, but returned to England in 1906. By now he had a sound knowledge of railway operating in difficult conditions, particularly on those with poorly laid track, sharp curves and steep gradients. It seems he had always been interested in the design of articulated locomotives and had carefully studied the features of Mallet, Meyer and Fairlie types, and also of the difficulties of raising steam in narrow gauge engines built with fireboxes restricted in width by the driving wheels.

He developed the idea that if the engine units were set clear of the boiler, the latter could be dropped low into the frames thus reducing the centre of gravity. This also allowed the boiler size to be be increased to almost the maximum permitted by the loading gauge. In a larger boiler a greater number of tubes could be fitted inside, and, equally important, the barrel could be shorter. The evaporative power of tubes decreases with length, so a larger number of short tubes is more efficient then fewer tubes of greater length, giving the same area of heating surface. Additionally, the fuel bunker and water tanks placed on top of the engine units enhance the adhesion and engine stability.

Back in England it is believed that Herbert Garratt continued to develop his ideas for articulated locomotives and in 1907 he offered Beyer Peacock at Gorton, Manchester, a specification for a two-foot gauge locomotive. The Tasmanian Government Railway had approached Beyer Peacock for a Mallet type. Garratt's scheme was modified to suit the Tasmanian requirements and so the first two Garratt locomotives were built at Gorton in 1909. They were compounds with cylinders placed on the inside end of the engine units with the low pressure cylinders on the front end. Little interest was taken at the time in this completely new locomotive concept, but in 1910 when Beyer Peacock built another two-foot gauge Garratt for the Darjeeling Himalayan Railway it obtained publicity in *The Locomotive* magazine. Following this, Beyer Peacock began to realise the potential of the market, albeit initially only for small narrow gauge locomotives.

Herbert Garratt died comparitively young in September 1913, but between 1909 and 1914 Beyer Peacock had built nine different designs of Garratt for five track gauges, totalling 31 locomotives. South Africa was to become a major purchaser of the type and it fell to the two-foot gauge railways to take delivery of the first Garratts in 1919, which were three 2-6-0+0-6-2s, classified NGG 11, and numbered NG51 to 53. These proved very satisfactory, so much so they influenced trials on the 3ft 6ins gauge of the SAR. Two more narrow gauge locomotives followed in 1925 and eventually a total of 63 two-foot gauge Garratts were built. It is to the credit to Herbert Garratt and Beyer Peacock that this design was in production for nearly sixty years and that the first and last of the type were built for two-foot gauge railways.

GARRATT CLASSES AND CLASS 91 LOCOMOTIVES

Loco No.	Class	Type	Builder	Works No.	Date
NG17	NG15	2-8-2	Hl	21905	1931
NG18	"	"	"	21906	1931
NG19	"	"	"	21907	1931
NG49	NGG13	2-6-2 + 2-6-2	Hg	10599	1928
NG50	"	"		10599	1928
NG51	NGG11	2-6-0 + 0-6-2	BP	5975	1919
NG52	"	"	"	5976	1919
NG53	"	"	"	5977	1919
NG54	"	"	"	6199	1925
NG55	"	"	"	6200	1925
NG56	NGG12	2-6-2 + 2-6-2	FB	2506	1927
NG57	"	"	"	2507	1927
NG58	NGG13	2-6-2 + 2-6-2		10549	1927
NG59	"	"	"	10550	1927
NG60	"	"	"	10551	1927
NG61	"	"	"	10552	1927
NG62	"	"	"	10553	1927
NG63	"	"	"	10554	1927
NG64	"	"	"	10555	1927
NG65	"	"	"	10556	1927
NG66	"	"	"	10557	1927
NG67	"	"	"	10558	1927
NG68	"	"	"	10559	1927
NG69	"	"	"	10560	1927
NG77	"	"	"	10629	1928
NG78	"	"	"	10630	1928
NG79	"	"	"	10631	1928
NG80	"	"	"	10632	1928
NG81	"	"	"	10633	1928
NG82	"	"	"	10634	1928
NG83	"	"	"	10635	1928
NG84	NGG14	2-6-2 + 2-6-2	Hg	10747	1928
NG85	NGG16	2-6-2 + 2-6-2	Cl	3265	1937
NG86	"	"	"	3266	1937
NG87	"	"	"	3267	1937
NG88	"	"	"	3268	1937
NG109	"	"	BP	6919	1937
NG110	"	"	"	6920	1937
NG111	"	"	"	6921	1937
NG112	"	"	"	6922	1937
NG113	"	"	"	6923	1937
NG114	"	"	"	6924	1937
NG115	"	"	"	6925	1937
NG116	"	"	"	6926	1937
NG117	NG15	2-8-2	Hl	24475	1938
NG118	"	"	"	24476	1938
NG119	"	"	"	24477	1938
NG120	"	"	FB	2667	1951
NG121	"	"	"	2668	1951
NG122	"	"	"	2669	1951
NG123	"	"	"	2670	1951
NG124	"	"	"	2671	1951
NG125	NGG16	2-6-2 + 2-6-2	BP	7426	1951
NG126	"	"	"	7427	1951
NG127	"	"	"	7428	1951
NG128	"	"	"	7429	1951
NG129	"	"	"	7430	1951
NG130	"	"	"	7431	1951
NG131	"	"	"	7432	1951
NG132	NG15	2-8-2	FB	2682	1952
NG133	"	"	"	2683	1952
NG134	"	"	"	2684	1952
NG135	"	"	"	2685	1952
NG136	"	"	"	2686	1952
E137	NGG16	2-6-2 + 2-6-2	BP	7862	1958
E138	"	"	"	7863	1958
E139	"	"	"	7864	1958
E140	"	"	"	7865	1958
E141	"	"	"	7866	1958
E142	"	"	"	7867	1958
E143	"	"	"	7868	1958
NG144	NG15	2-8-2	Hl	29585	1957
NG145	"	"	"	29586	1957
NG146	"	"	"	29587	1957
NG147	"	"	"	29588	1957
NG148	"	"	"	29589	1957
NG149	NGG16	2-6-2 + 2-6-2	HT	3894	1967
NG150	"	"	"	3895	1967
NG151	"	"	"	3896	1968
NG152	"	"	"	3897	1968
NG153	"	"	"	3898	1968
NG154	"	"	"	3899	1968
NG155	"	"	"	3900	1968
NG156	"	"	"	3901	1968
91-001 to 91-020	91	Bo-Bo UM6B 700 hp	GE	38603- 38622	1973

Locomotive Builders

BP	=	Beyer Peacock	Beyer, Peacock & Co Ltd., Manchester
Cl	=	Cockerill	Societe John Cockerill, Seraing, Belgium
FB	=	Franco Belge	Soc. Franco Belge, La Croyere & Raismes
GE	=	General Electric	General Electric, Erie, Pennsylvania
Hg	=	Hanomag	Hannoversche Maschinenbau AG, Hannover
Hl	=	Henschel	Henschel & Sohn, Kassel
HT	=	Hunslet Taylor	Hunslet Taylor & Co (Pty) Ltd, Johannesburg

ACKNOWLEDGEMENTS

In addition to those mentioned in the photographic credits, I have received much help from the following, for which I thank them: Terry Bagworth, Peter Burton, Paul Catchpole, Mike Cotterell, Norman Langridge, Colin Marsden, Vic Mitchell, Charles Parry, David Payling and Mark Robinson. I am particularly grateful to Bruno Martin, now living in Queensland, for information and many of the maps in this album, which he has so carefully produced for me.

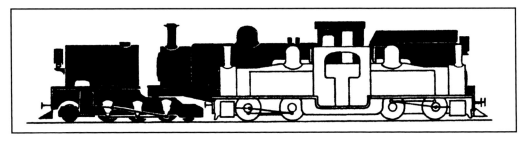

Diagram of a Ffestiniog Railway Fairlie superimposed on a class NGG13 Garratt.
(S.M.Moir/reproduced courtesy of Oakwood Press)

British Isles compared with South Africa.

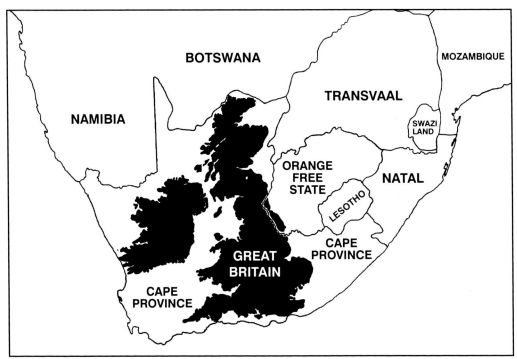

Weenen - Estcourt Railway

1. WEENEN – ESTCOURT

This branch was the most northerly of the five SAR two-foot gauge railways. It was opened in 1907 to connect the small town of Weenen, situated in an important vegetable and citrus fruit growing district of Natal, with Estcourt a town on the main line from Durban to Johannesburg. It was 29 miles long and the usual working was for a daily mixed train from Weenen departing about 08.15 and returning from Estcourt in the afternoon, with an extra train as required, particularly during the vegetable season. Two NNG13 class Garratts were allocated to the railway, the operational engine being stabled at Weenen and the relief at Estcourt, with engine changes every 20 working days with boiler wash-out and maintenance carried out at Estcourt. Weenen station was set in a very neat and tidy location on the western edge of the town with a small engine and a turning triangle. On leaving the station the railway ran alongside the main Greytown to Ladysmith road for two miles before changing direction and climbing around sharp bends and reverse curves to bridge the River Nathanguo before reaching Mona station, 640 feet above Weenen. The line then continued in a more south-westerly direction twisting and turning on its way to the highest point of the railway at Haviland, situated in open country, four thousand feet above sea level. Continuing southwards there were views across the hills and valleys and at Peniston, 22 miles from Weenen, the line dropped sharply to cross the main Durban to Johannesburg road before coming towards Estcourt and into the station alongside the main line. Estcourt is nearly one thousand feet higher than Weenen and the railway had gradients of 1 in 33 and curves of 200 feet radius.

In the early 1970s the two NGG13 class Garratts allocated were nos. 60 and 78 and were kept in immaculate condition. About this time passenger numbers declined, but the mixed train continued to run and by 1978 NGG13 no.78 in blue livery, carrying a headboard *The Liliputian* was in regular use. NGG11 no.55, also in blue, and NGG13 no.78 completed the allocation. Other locomotives reported on this line included NGG13 nos.59 and 77. In 1981 no. 59 was badly damaged when it overturned working a Weenen bound mixed train and no.78 was the replacement. By 1982 the train only ran three days a week, later reduced to an 'as required' service, and eventually the railway was closed on 31st August 1983.

WEENEN

↑   1.1   NGG13 class Garratt no.78 is standing outside Weenen shed being prepared to work the daily mixed train to Estcourt on 23rd July 1981. (Roger Siviter)

←   1.2   Seen in June 1977, we note the end veranda first class coach number 4 is on the rear of the mixed train standing at the platform. Marshalled in front of it is a composite brake and a third class composite coach.
(Brian Manktelow)

1.3   On static display on 31st July 1980 was NGG11 Garratt no. 55 built by Beyer Peacock in 1925, one of the five original Garratts supplied for the South African narrow gauge lines. This locomotive was removed from Weenen in 2003 and overhauled at Sandstone Estates in 2004 to work on the Paton's Country Railway at Ixopo.
(Roger Siviter)

➔   1.4   NGG13 Garratt no. 78 is in spotless condition in this picture taken on 23rd July 1981, and is brewing up and making ready to leave with the mixed train to Estcourt. The locomotive is carrying the head-board *Liliputian* on the front tank.
(Roger Siviter)

↗   1.5   Five years earlier another NGG13 class, no. 59, was painted in blue livery and is seen with its well known regular driver, Mr. Billy Bester in charge, pulling out of the station in 1976. (David C Rodgers)

NEW FARROW

1.6   At the first crossing loop, barely a mile from Weenen, Billy Bester is bringing NGG13 no. 78 through the loop with an Estcourt bound train on 23rd July 1981. (Roger Siviter)

1.7   NGG13 no. 59, seen in 1976, is getting into its stride on the relatively level section after leaving the loop and before starting the climb towards Mona. (David C Rodgers)

MONA

1.8   This picture was taken in June 1977 and gives us a view of Garratt no. 59 coming onto the lattice steel girder bridge over the River Nathangwa, near the station, six miles from Weenen, en route to Estcourt. (Brian Manktelow)

MIELIETUIN

1.9   Driver Billy Bester starts Garratt no. 78 away from the loop with the daily mixed train from Weenen on 1st August 1980. (Roger Siviter)

1.10   Looking south from the loop in June 1977, NGG13 no. 59 pulls away across the unmade dirt road on its way towards Estcourt. Unfortunately, this engine was written off following an accident, in which the fireman was killed, in January 1982. (Brian Manktelow).

ESTCOURT

1.11   NGG13 no. 78 is being serviced near the coaling stage after arrival from Weenen on 1st August 1980. (Roger Siviter)

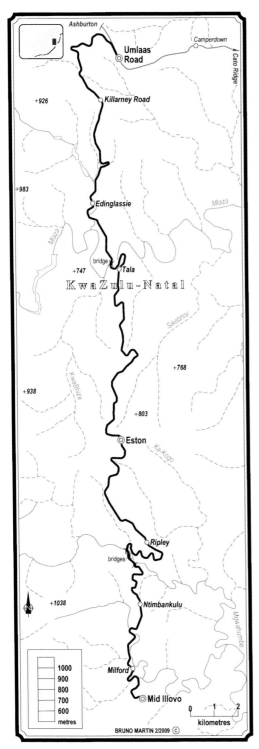

Umlaas Road - Mid Illovo Railway

2. UMLAAS ROAD - MID ILLOVO

In 1902 a survey was made to construct a two-foot gauge railway between Umlass Road and Mid Illovo, but work to build the railway did not commence until March 1909 and the line officially opened on 12th April 1911. Umlass Road is situated on the main Durban to Johannesberg electrified line 50 miles from Durban and is at an elevation of 2606 feet above sea level.

The railway was 27½ miles long and passed throught some of the finest agricultural land in KwaZulu Natal. Besides the requirements of a rural community, the railway mainly carried cattle, fertiliser, timber and wattle bark, the latter being used in the tanning industry. In the 1970s there were three NGG13 class Garratts allocated working from the small shed at Umlass Road. The regular train service provided was a weekday mixed train which left Umlass Road at 05.30 and was booked to arrive Mid Illovo at 08.45. After shunting and servicing, the return train departed at 09.30 with an arrival due back at Umlass Road at 12.40. In practice this timetable was very difficult to observe as it did not allow enough time for intermediate shunting, so late running was not unusual. Except in the earliest days of the railway there were no turning facitities at Mid Illovo, and the practice was for the engine to run out from Umlass Road bunker first. The maximum train load was 200 tons.

The narrow gauge line started northwards out of Umlass Road station and made a 180 degree turn southwards and descended at 1 in 40 into a valley by means of a horseshoe curve, passing a siding at Killarney Road. More steep gradients, rock cutting and curves, another siding at Edinglassie, all followed before coming down into the valley of the Umlass River. Here the locomotive would take water from a large concrete tank near Tala and the train then crossed the river on a 560ft long bridge 30ft above the water level. From here there was another uphill slog, again on 1 in 40, towards Eston, at just over 15 miles, the only intermediate station and highest point at 2619 feet above sea level on the branch. The railway continued up and down through varied open rural scenery and woodland, often still on 1 in 40 gradients, and passed sidings at Ripley, Ntimbankulu and Milford before ascending a sharp right hand curve into the terminus at Mid Illovo.

The railway was officially closed on 28th February 1985 but a last 'Farmers Special' was run on 9th March 1985.

UMLAAS ROAD

2.1   The very small narrow gauge loco shed was alongside the electrified main line to Durban, which is visible on the left. The Garratt on the right has just returned with the daily mixed train from Mid Illovo, and is about to retreat into the shed for 'disposal' at the end of the working day in 1973. (Bruno Martin)

2.2   NGG13 no.59, built by Hanomag in 1927 is taking water near the shed and was photographed on 2nd November 1971. (John K Williams)

TALA

2.3   Caught on camera in October 1981 in open country, NGG13 no.77 is seen slogging up the 1 in 40 climb from Tala towards Eston with the daily train from Umlass Road to Mid Illovo. (Dick Manton)

ESTON

2.4   NGG13 no.77 is nearing the station, in October 1981, with the Mid Illovo bound goods. At the time this engine was distinctive with a blue painted boiler and frames, whilst its bunker and tank retained the standard black livery. (Dick Manton)

2.5   Four years later, on 23rd February 1985, no.77 is arriving with one of the last scheduled trains en route to Umlass Road. Travelling at the back of the train were a group of Railway Society of Southern Africa, Natal Branch members making a farewell journey to commemorate the passing of 74 years of continuous service of this steam worked line. (Bruno Martin)

2.6   In October 1981, no. 77 is seen pulling away from the station with the daily mixed train to Mid Illovo having dropped off some of the wagons in the siding at this station. (Dick Manton)

SOUTH OF ESTON

2.7   The same train as shown in picture 2.5 is now in open country passing native huts on its way to Umlass Road. (Bruno Martin)

2.8   Passing some woodland, Garratt no.77 is seen nine years earlier, in June 1976, with another loaded train bound for Umlass Road. (Terence M Bagworth)

MID ILLOVO

2.9   This is the end of the branch, nearly 27½ miles from Umlass Road and at an elevation 2363ft above sea level. NGG13 no. 59 is standing at the platform in 1973. (Bruno Martin)

3. UMZINTO - DONNYBROOK

This two-foot gauge line was built to serve Alexandra County and the Ixopo District, and originally known as the 'Stuartstown Railway', which was the former name of Ixopo. The well known railway contractor, Pauling & Co. Ltd was awarded the contract to build the railway from Esperanza (on the 3ft 6ins gauge south coast branch line to Umzinto) to Donnybrook, a distance of 96½ miles. Work started in 1906 but progress was hampered by the seasonal heavy rains which are a feature of this part of Natal, and caused washouts to the new formation. In April 1908 just before the railway was ready for its final inspection a torrential downpour caused considerable damage and the railway was not opened for traffic until 3rd June 1908. On the upper section the narrow gauge joined the Cape-Natal railway 2½ miles south of Donnybrook, so a third rail was laid into the station. Likewise at the coastal end a third rail was laid from Esperanza to Umzinto, a distance of 1¼ miles.

In its 97 miles, the railway rose from near sea level to over 4500 feet above sea level near Eastwolds, necessitating a ruling gradient of 1 in 33.3. The line passed through extremely attractive countryside containing deep river valleys and rolling hills. The first part of the inland journey, where the climate and vegetation is sub-tropical, was through sugar cane fields. After some 30 miles this changed to open farmland and timber plantations. The railway had a beneficial effect on farming although at the time of opening in 1908 there was a ban on the movement of cattle due to an outbreak of East Coast Fever. Other main commodities carried were maize, wool, timber, bark and, in the 1920s, milk to the South African Condensed Milk Factory at Donnybrook. The original train service consisted of one mixed train each weekday between between Umzinto and Ixopo and a four-days a week service between Ixopo and Donnybrook.

On 2nd February 1914, a branch line 17 ½ miles long was opened from Union Bridge Junction, just north of Ixopo to Madonela. South from Ixopo the line climbed to its highest point at Stainton, 3720 feet above sea level and four miles from the junction. From here it descended over the remaining 13 miles to Madonela, 2458 feet above sea level. Until the 1960s this was a busy line with cattle traffic and Madonela station receipts were the best of the railway.

This branch was closed because of washaways on 12th September 1985, but in November 2000 part of the branch was used again by Paton's Mini Express with a gangers trolley! Nine miles of the branch between Allwoodburn (just south of Ixopo) and Ncalu, is now operated by Paton's Country Narrow Gauge Railway using, on occasions, the venerable NGG11 Garratt no.55, built by Beyer Peacock in 1925.

The Umzinto to Highflats section was breached by a tropical storm on 29th January 1984 and officially closed in May/June 1985. This was followed by Highflats to Ixopo closing on 20th September 1985 and finally between Ixopo and Donnybrook on 30th June 1986, although a last special train ran for the benefit of local people on 12th July 1986.

Donnybrook - Umzinto Railway

UMZINTO

3.1   A scene at the shed dated 5th April 1970, showing no less than seven NGG16 class Garratts, all in gleaming condition. On the right right there is nos.114, 152, 150 and 115, centre nos. 87 and 113, and then no. 85 on the left side of the picture. (Chris Gammell/Peter Lemmey coll.)

3.2   The high level coaling stage was very much a feature of South African locomotive shed facilities, even on some of the narrow gauge lines, and this shows coal being discharged into the bunker of Garratt no.131 in June 1977. (Brian Manktelow)

BRAEMAR

GLEN ROSA

3.3 Climbing steadily into the hills and already over 1300 feet above sea level but less than fifteen miles from Umzinto, NGG16 no. 85, the first of the class was seen on 5th April 1970 at the head of a long train of empty wagons bound for Ixopo. (Chris Gammell/Peter Lemmey coll.)

3.4 On 14th August 1981 passing sugar cane fields, Garratt no. 113 is coming upgrade with the 07.25 goods from Umzinto to Ixopo. (Author)

3.5 A little later on the 14th August 1981, the train seen in picture 3.4 is coming around a hillside towards the station. (Author)

3.6　Pictured on the same day, having taken on water from the water gantry, NGG16 no.113 starts away from the station with the 07.25 goods to Ixopo. This station was just twenty miles from Umzinto and 1957 feet above sea level. (Author)

↗ 3.7　As sometimes happens, wheels do occasionally become derailed and here is a spot of trouble with NGG16 no.113. The front pony wheels have come off the track and this shows the front end jacked-up and re-railing in progress before the train proceeded onwards to Ixopo. This mishap happened on 10th August 1976. (Roger Siviter)

MBUBULA

3.8   Six miles beyond, Glen Rosa on 14th August 1981 no. 113 is pulling out of the loop and continuing uphill towards Ixopo. (Author)

DUMISA

3.9　　NGG16 no.129 is heading a short goods train from Umzinto to Ixopo on 10th August 1976. This locomotive is on the Puffing Billy Railway, Victoria (Austrilia), but will need re-gauging to 2ft 6ins before it can be used. (Roger Siviter)

JOLIVET

3.10　　Looking down from the nearby main road in June 1977, the scene includes one of the Hunslet-Taylor built Garratts, no. 150, coming along the hillsides and curving on its way uphill towards Ixopo. (Brian Manktelow)

HLATANKUNGU

3.11   A view from 9th August 1976 shows how the railway wound its way through the attractive rolling hills and, in this area, sugar cane growing country, as the little Garratt no.129 comes downhill with a timber train en route from Ixopo to Umzinto. (Roger Siviter)

HIGHFLATS

3.12   In June 1977 NGG16 no.150 was seen leaving the village with a timber train bound for Umzinto. (Brian Manktelow)

3.13   Crossing a different bridge in the same area on 16th August 1969, is another NGG16, also bringing a timber train downhill en route to Umzinto. (Basil Roberts/Peter Lemmey coll.)

IXOPO

3.14   NGG16 no.113 is approaching the town with a train of empties working as the 07.25 goods from Umzinto to Ixopo on 14th August 1981. This town was the main intermediate point on the railway and nearby was the junction for the Madonela branch. It is nearly 68 miles from Umzinto and 3257 feet above sea level. (Author)

3.15   A general view of the loco shed which had just been rebuilt, with three NGG16s standing outside on 4th August 1970; left to right nos, 140, 151 and 86. (Chris Gammell/Peter Lemmey coll.)

3.16   A close-up view taken on 14th August 1981, is of two Garratts standing in the afternoon sunlight outside the shed; left is no.143 and no.109 right. (Author)

VAUSE

3.17   From here there was a very steep climb, much of it at 1 in 33.3 for six miles towards Crystal Manor and this shows a Garratt working hard climbing upgrade in the evening sunlight on 14th August 1981, en route to Donnybrook. (Author)

LUFAFA ROAD

3.18   Following the official closing of the railway in June 1986, a last special was organised for local people. The train hauled by Garratt no.113 on 12th July 1986, is seen on its return from Ixopo back to Donnybrook. (Tony Eaton)

MAXWELL

3.19   On 21st March 1986 NGG16 no.87 is seen passing the station with the 06.00 train from Ixopo to Donnybrook. This engine is now on the Welsh Highland Railway, having been restored by the Ffestiniog Railway at Boston Lodge Works in January 2009. (Dick Manton)

DONNYBROOK JUNCTION

3.20 This is the dual-gauge track with the two-foot gauge rails moving off the 3ft 6ins line onto its own right of way, looking south. (Bruno Martin)

DONNYBROOK

3.21 Gleaming in the morning sunlight on 12th July 1986, NGG16 no. 113 is seen being prepared to work the very last train, a special for local people, which was a return trip to Ixopo. (Tony Eaton)

3.22 There was a small narrow gauge shed, as seen here, where NGG16 no.87 is receiving attention and taking water outside on 21st March 1986. (Dick Manton)

4. PORT SHEPSTONE - HARDING
Alfred County Railway

An inland area south of Durban known as 'No-mans land' sandwiched between the Zulu and Xhosa peoples was annexed by Natal in 1866 and named Alfred County after Prince Alfred, the younger son of Queen Victoria. Because of the difficult and rugged countryside a two-foot gauge railway was chosen to develop the region. The first 24 miles to Paddock was opened in 1911, to Izingolwini 37 miles in 1915 and, finally to Harding 76 miles by 1917. The railway passed through most attractive country of southern Kwa Zulu ranging from rolling green hills and valleys to mountainous scenery. The farmers found the railway of great benefit and transport of agricultural produce, timber, bananas and, later sugar cane and pulp wood, became important scources of revenue.

Passenger traffic was light and withdrawn in 1963 and in 1986 the railway was closed by SA Transport Services (the successors to SAR in 1981). This led to the formation of the Alfred County Railway by Messrs Charlie Lewis and Alan Jorgensen in an attempt to save the railway and generate new business, particularly the carriage of timber. Agreement was reached with SATS in December 1987 for the ACR to operate a steam worked freight railway.

The ACR directors played a leading role in raising capital for the repair and reinstatement of the whole line, unprecedented in South Africa, as a private railway undertaking was unknown. The service started, using only Garratts, and the first train to Harding was hauled by no. 88 ran on 28th March 1988. Strenerous efforts were made to increase traffic and by 1989 eight Garratts and over 160 wagons had been refurbished. The company expended much effort in providing the type of wagons needed to carry timber, the mainstay traffic, and also in improving transhippment facilities. A mechcanical engineer, Phil Girdlestone, from the Ffestiniog Railway, joined the railway to introduce gas-producer firing and other refinements to the Garratts, in order to improve efficiency. In 1992, due to the cost of maintaining water supplies on the upper sections of the line, two class 91 diesels were hired from Spoornet (the successor to S A Transport Services), but steam continued to be used on the Banana Express and the section below Paddock. The company suffered increasing problems, not least, against competition by road hauliers carrying timber, with regards to lorry sizes and unfair subsidies, and despite the popularity of the Banana Express, services were suspended in April 2006 and the railway closed.

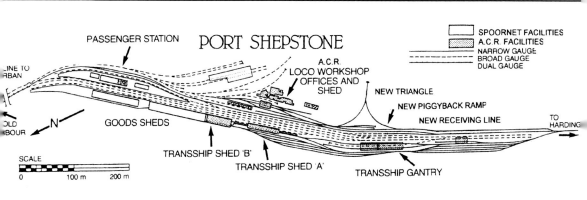

PORT SHEPSTONE

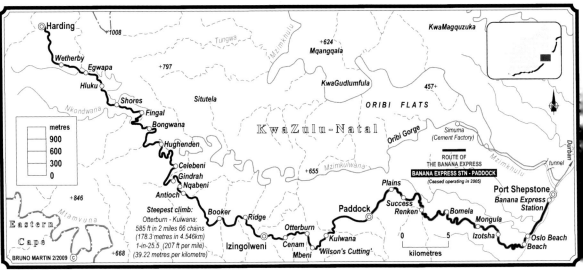

Port Shepstone - Harding Railway (1917-1986)

Alfred County Railway (1988-2006)

4.1　　A general view of the dual gauge yard and some of the extensive sidings looking south is from September 1992. Centre is the narrow-gauge locomotive shed and, to its left, the 3ft 6ins gauge siding serving the loco fueling point. (Vic Mitchell)

4.2   This view, photographed in September 1992, gives us sight of the narrow-gauge shed and 3ft 6ins gauge siding alongside, with Spoornet diesel no.36-229 stabled on it. This makes a good comparison with the 2ft gauge no.91-006, on hire to the Alfred County Railway. Despite the track gauge difference, it has a similar loading gauge to the 36 class diesel. For transfer from Port Elizabeth it was placed on 3ft 6ins bogies and came here in September 1992 under its own power. (Vic Mitchell)

SOUTH OF PORT SHEPSTONE

4.3   Just getting into its stride on leaving Port Shepstone on 13th August 1981, no.141 is crossing a creek with the 09.00 train to Harding. (Author)

➜   4.4   Coming south out of Port Shepstone the railway follows the Indian Ocean coast for four miles passing Dawn View Hotel (formerly Beach Terminus) before turning inland near Shelly Beach towards Izotsha. Here no.110, in green livery, is working the 13.10 from Port Shepstone to Harding on 13th August 1981. (Author)

4.5   Near to where picture 4.4 was taken on 13th August 1981, Garratt no.142 is seen in
evening light on the last stages of its journey with a timber train from Harding. (Author)

4.6   Photographed on 14th August 1986, a few weeks before closure by SAR, NGG16 no. 138 crosses the Izotsha Creek Bridge near Shelly Beach with the 10.15 goods train to Harding. This bridge was of 8-span steel girder construction supported on cast-iron screw piles which resist rust, and are vitually indestructible. (Author)

4.7   The main road to Shelly Beach and railway run parallel to the coast as seen here on 13th August 1981, with green liveried Garratt no.110 heading inland with the 13.10 goods train from Port Shepstone. (Author)

4.8 and 4.9   The management of the Alfred County Railway actively promoted their tourist train which regularly ran from Port Shepstone to Izotsha, a journey of eight miles each way. On occasions, additional trains ran further up-country to Paddock, a distance 24 miles. In conjunction with their train the company produced some attractive postcards and this and the following picture are views of the train, hauled by a green painted Garratt, with the Indian Ocean in the background. (Vic Mitchell coll.)

IZOTSHA

4.10   Rumbling into the station on 14th August 1986, NGG16 Garratt no.138 (now working on the Welsh Highland Railway) came slowly into view with the 10.15 train from Port Shepstone to Harding. (Author)

BOMELA

4.11   From Izotsha the hard work began with gradients as steep as 1 in 37 and here NGG16 no.110 is working hard towards the station with the 13.10 train to Harding on 13th August 1986. (Author)

4.12   Again on 13th August 1986, the same locomotive as seen in the previous picture is arriving at the station with the 13.10 train from Port Shepstone to Harding. (Author)

4.13.   Hardly an appropriate headboard for a train of bogie water tank wagons, albeit a vital commodity, seen on the front tank of no.88 as it left the station on its way to Paddock in this photograph dated 13th August 1986. (Author)

RENKEN

4.14   This station was nearly 18 miles from Port Shepstone 1161 feet above sea level and is seen with NGG16 no.88 pausing in the loop with its train of water tanks on 13th August 1986. (Author)

4.15   Following the water tank train a few hours later on the same day, Garratt no.110 is seen with empty timber wagons being returned to Izingolweni and Harding. (Author)

PADDOCK

4.16   Another picture taken on 13th August 1986, in attractive scenery on the climb towards Paddock, no.110 is still working hard with its train of empty wagons. (Author)

4.17   This station is 1685 feet above sea level and had been declared a national monument so the Alfred County Railway produced this postcard in recognition and that, on occasions, the "Banana Express" came here. (Vic Mitchell coll.)

4.18   Again on 13th August 1986, no. 88 having shunted and delivered its train of full water tanks is now ready to return to Port Shepstone with three empties and its bogie composite brake van as soon as the next uphill train arrives. (Author)

4.19   Garratt no.110 is seen entering the station whilst green liveried no.88 stands in the loop waiting to return to Port Shepstone on 13th August 1986. (Author)

4.20   Still carrying its "Banana Express" headboard on that day, no.88 comes over the points and out of the loop at the start of its journey back to Port Shepstone. (Author)

WILSONS CUTTING

4.21   After Paddock the railway followed a switchback course and at this photogenic location inland bound trains had a short spell of downhill running before resuming more uphill work to Izingolweni. Here on 13th August 1981, no.142 is seen working the 06.45 train from Port Shepstone to Harding. (Author)

← 4.22 Nearly half way to Harding the climb continued in a rural setting, passing many villages and settlements with their traditional Zulu huts as seen in the next three pictures. Garratt no.155 had a light load for Harding on 12th August 1981. (Author)

← 4.23 In this photograph of 13th August 1986, no. 110 with an SAR emblem on the front tank is seen hauling the 11.00 goods from Port Shepstone. (Author)

4.24 Negotiating a reverse curve, no. 155 was photographed near Izingolweni on 12th August 1981. (Author)

WEST OF IZINGOLWENI

4.25   Izingolweni station was just over 37 miles from Port Shepstone and 1900ft above sea level, but the railway still continued climbing towards Harding. On 12th August 1981, having dropped off some wagons at Izingolweni, no.155 is seen on its way towards its final destination, Harding, 76 miles from Port Shepstone. (Author)

EAST OF HARDING

4.26   In July 1986, still climbing in open high country, an NGG16 Garratt is seen with a train of empties bound for Harding and passing some of the many traditional native huts found in this area. (Tony Eaton)

HARDING

4.27   Photographed in September 1992, the station building was of substantial construction with a raised platform. It is just under 76 miles from Port Shepstone and its elevation was stated to be 2885 feet above sea level. (Vic Mitchell)

4.28   The locomotive shed had two roads, and visible on 12th August 1981 were NGG16 class Garratts no.154 and on the right no.88. (Author)

5. PORT ELIZABETH – AVONTUUR

including the Patensie Branch

This is the longest of the five SAR two-foot gauge lines featured in this album being just over 177 miles from Port Elizabeth, to Avontuur; compare this with a two-foot gauge train journey in England from Paddington to just beyond Exeter!

The railway was opened in stages from 23rd December 1903 and finally to Avontuur three years later on 10th December 1906. The line generally follows an east-west course parallel to the south-east coast of Cape Province, but separated by a mountain range. Famous for fruit growing, particularly apples, the region is known as the Lang Kloof. In 1914 a branch line 17 miles long was opened from Gamtoos along the Gamtoos river valley to Patensie and in 1927 a private siding from Chelsea, 12 miles long, was built to bring limestone down from Patensie, and later Loerie, to the cement works of the Eastern Province Cement Company at New Brighton. The Avontuur railway proved extremely useful to the farmers in the Lang Kloof and enabled them to transport their fruit and vegetables to markets in Port Elizabeth and for a substantial export business, especially apples and pears. In addition, the transport of limestone, timber and later, charcoal, was also important. With the increasing freight, and the tight curves of the track, it was apparent that articulated locomotives with greater power and flexibility would be advantageous, thus in 1919 Beyer Peacock supplied SAR with three Garratts. These locomotives were classified as NGG11 and one, no.NG51, came to the Avontuur line in 1920 with the other two going up to Natal. Having proved its worth NG51 joined its sisters in Natal but in 1928 seven new Hanomag built NGG13 class Garratts came to this railway and were an instant success. A modified series, NGG16 built in 1937, initially saw three allocated to the line and more Garratts were subsequently drafted in during following years. In addition to the Garratts, 21 class NG15 2-8-2s which had been transferred from South West Africa in 1960,

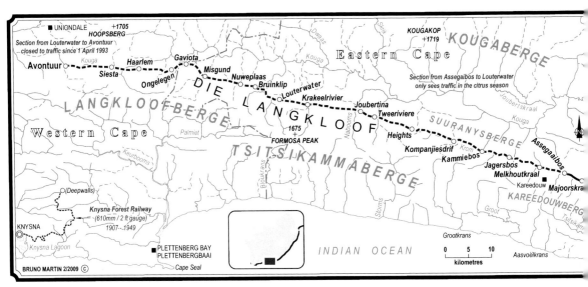

Humewood Road - Avontuur 2 ft./610 mm gauge railway

and class 91 diesels arriving in 1973, provided the railways motive power.

1965 saw the beginnings of a tourist service when the Port Elizabeth Historical Society organised a train and, SAR recognising the potential, started a monthly excursion from Port Elizabeth to Loerie, a distance of 44½ miles which included a run over Van Stadens Bridge, the highest two-foot gauge railway bridge in the world, 254 feet above the river. In 1993 SAR, by now Spoornet, decided the passenger trains should be run by a private operator and the Alfred County Railway took over and ran the trains more successfully than Spoornet. Even so, the ACR management decided in 1995 they could not continue and the 'Apple Express Society' was formed in August 1995 with the backing of the Transnet Heritage Foundation. The Society established a service of tourist trains to Thornhill, 33 miles, then to Loerie with special trains, and if pre-booked, further up the Lang Kloof and also the Patensie branch. Spoornet subsequently introduced a 'steam exit plan' which required steam operators to disband and reform as a 'Section 21 Company' – a not for profit company under section 21 of the South African Companies Act. The Society formed the 'Port Elizabeth Apple Express' company and continued to run passenger trains and in 2008 was allowed to use the railway as far as Assegaaibos, 100 miles, and the Patensie branch. The line west of Assegaaibos was closed at the end of 2007 due to heavy rain but in 2008 a diesel hauled train was able to reach Louterwater, 144 miles, so there was hope that this section would reopen in 2009. Meanwhile Spoornet was running timber trains with their class 91 diesels approximately once a week and the Apple Express was running three or four times each month. During 2009 it was expected the Apple Express would be hauled by NG15 no.119 and possibly NGG16 Garratt no.131.

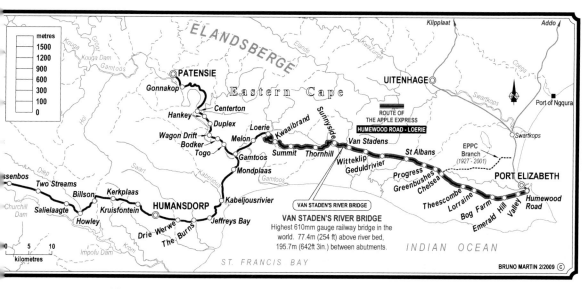

Humewood Road - Avontuur 2 ft./610 mm gauge railway
Humewood Road - Essenbos section and branch line to Patensie

PORT ELIZABETH

5.1   On 19th October 1969 vintage locomotives on two gauges were seen in the loco shed yard. Left is NGG11 Garratt no.54, built by Beyer Peacock in 1925 and on 3ft 6ins gauge is class 6 4-6-0 no.429 built by Dubs in 1894, having its tender tank filled with water. Behind on the right, a more modern S2 class 0-8-0, built by Krupp in 1952 can be seen shunting.
(Basil Roberts/Peter Lemmey coll.)

5.2   This view on 31st March 1970, shows part of the extensive dual gauge yards where the venerable Garratt no.54 is shunting across some 3ft 6ins gauge sidings.
(Chris Gammell/Peter Lemmey coll.)

5.3   NGG13 Garratt no.83, built by Hanomag in 1928, is marshalling its train in the narrow gauge yard on 30th March 1970. This locomotive is now preserved in Germany.
(Chris Gammell/Peter Lemmey coll.)

5.4　A two-foot gauge Garratt hauls a train of vans across the 3ft 6ins tracks on 29th April 1973. Open and covered exchange sidings are on the right. Both gauges ran into a joint passenger terminus behind the camera until the 1930s. (David J Mitchell)

←　5.5　In its earlier days of operation, the "Apple Express" received no special recognition, as seen here, when it pulled out of the yard in September 1972.
(Tony Eaton)

5.6   On 26th July 1980, eight years later, more commercial enterprise is apparent as the locomotive now has a distinctive headboard, insignia on its smoke deflectors and is well cleaned, as it comes out from the station with the "Apple Express". The narrow gauge loco shed is visible on the right. (Roger Siviter)

5.7   Humewood Road narrow gauge station looking south on 19th March 1997, includes wagons sheeted over, carrying empty orange boxes awaiting return to Patensie. (Vic Mitchell)

5.8   By 1997 the veteran NGG11 Garratt no. 54 was seldom used, but on the evening of 19th March 1997 it is shown backing into the station prior to taking a Ffestiniog Travel party for a short evening excursion to Chelsea. (Vic Mitchell)

CHELSEA

5.9   NG15 no.136 is seen arriving at the station on 30th October 1971 with a passenger train. Note the coaching stock is painted in what for many years was the standard SAR livery of red and light grey. This station is 14 miles from Port Elizabeth and already 668 feet above sea level. (John K Williams)

5.10   This was the junction for the private siding of the Pretoria Portland Cement Co (previously the Eastern Province Cement Co) which went 12 miles to the cement factory at New Brighton, near Port Elizabeth. Viewed on 29th October 1971, 2-8-2 no.121 is shunting at the exchange sidings, whilst in the background loaded limestone wagons from Loerie are waiting to go forward down to the factory. This locomotive went on to be privately preserved at Hambledon in England.
(John K Williams)

VAN STADENS BRIDGE

5.11   In July 1986, very appropriately, the Apple Express NG15 locomotive and the coaching stock was painted green, and this attractive train is seen crossing the impressive bridge over Van Stadens Gorge. This bridge has 11 spans totalling 632 feet and is 254 feet above water level. (Tony Eaton)

THORNHILL

5.12   Taken eight years before the previous picture in July 1978, immaculate NG15 no.144 in black livery, also looks most impressive as it brings the 'Apple Express' from Port Elizabeth into the station. (Author)

SUMMIT

5.13   NG15 no.144 is again seen in July 1978 with the 'Apple Express' approaching the station.
Although called 'Summit' it was 747 feet above sea level and 37 miles from Port Elizabeth, whereas
the highest point between Humewood Road and Loerie was 837ft at Sunnyside, 29½ miles. Even
so, from Summit the line dropped nearly 650 feet in eight miles to Loerie on a ruling gradient of 1
in 40, plus numerous reverse curves which presented a formidable obstacle for drivers of eastbound
trains. (Author)

LOERIE

5.14   Standing in the loop in October 1968 and facing the 1 in 40 climb from the station, NG15 no. 145 is waiting to leave with a train to Port Elizabeth. Forty years later this locomotive was still at Humewood Road, but out of service. (David J Mitchell)

5.15   Looking in the opposite direction to the previous picture on 30th October 1971, double headed NG15s nos.134 & 145 enter the station with a goods train from Port Elizabeth. No.134 is now on the Welsh Highland Railway. (John K Williams)

5.16 In 1934 the Eastern Province Cement Company opened a quarry at Limebank, about seven miles away, and the crushed limestone was carried in bulk on an overhead ropeway to the railway at Loerie. Sidings were built alongside the loading bunker at the end of the ropeway. In 1954 when the quarry output was doubled, a second parallel ropeway and bunker was built, seen here, and was in use until May 2000, when the quarry became worked out. This photograph is from 20th March 1997. (Vic Mitchell)

ASSEGAAIBOS

➔ 5.17 This station is just over one hundred miles from Port Elizabeth and had engine servicing facilities and a railway settlement. This view, as recorded on film on 24th June 1977, shows part of the loco shed with four engines standing outside. These are from right to left nos. 121, 122, 119 and 147. (Author)

➘ 5.18 On 24th June 1977 NG15 no.147 is seen having its tender filled with water. Note that the fireman is standing on an improvised wooden platform designed to assist him reaching the water valve. (Author)

TWO RIVERS

← 5.19 This picture from 24th June 1977 shows a feature once sometimes used on locomotives in some hot African and Asian countries, but unknown in the United Kingdom. Where space is limited and conditions become very hot, the ability to sit outside the cab makes the work more bearable and this picture shows the driver's seat swung outside the cab. Note also the red fire-guard to protect the drivers legs from the heat of the firebox, especially when the door is opened for firing. On the cabside is a standard SAR brass numberplate showing the name in English around the top edge and Africaans around the bottom edge, with loco number in the middle and class designation in small letters immediately underneath. (Author)

← 5.20 From Assegaaibos the railway, with small exceptions, is climbing continuously and in the last thirty miles has risen 1050 feet to this station where NG15 no.17 has arrived on 24th June 1977 with the 07.15 train from Assegaaibos to Avontuur. (Author)

5.21 The same train as in picture 5.20 leaves the station. This locomotive went to the Sandstone Railway near Ficksburg in the Orange Free State. (Author)

JOUBERTINA

5.22   In an attractive setting on 24th June 1977, 2-8-2 no.17 comes into the station with the 07.15 train to Avontuur. (Author)

5.23   NGG13 class, Garratt no.80, built by Hanomag in 1932, is seen preserved at the station on 24th June 1977. (Author)

5.24   NG15 no.147 leaves the station on the same day with the 04.00 goods train from Avontuur to Assegaaibos. (Author)

TOWARDS LOUTERWATER

5.25   This picture taken on 24th June 1977 shows the attractive scenery as the railway continues climbing towards Avontuur. No.17 is hauling the 07.15 train from Assegaaibos. (Author)

NUWEPLAAS

5.26   NG15 no.17 is coming cautiously into the station on 24th June 1977 with its train to Avontuur, whilst sister engine no.18 waits in the loop to depart with the 12.00 train from Misgund to Asssegaaibos. (Author)

5.27   This view on the same day at the western end of the station has both trains waiting to leave in opposite directions. The station is 150½ miles from Port Elizabeth and 2400ft above sea level. (Author)

IN THE LANG KLOOF

5.28   The next four pictures show trains, on the 24th June 1977, in the valley of the Lang Kloof, all taken over 2400ft above sea level towards the western end of the railway. This is no.147 coming down grade with the 04.00 train from Avontuur to Assegaaibos. (Author)

5.29   Further down the valley NG15 no.147 is making steady progress towards Assegaaibos. (Author)

5.30　No.17 is seen crossing the main road on its way to Avontuur, with the mountains forming an imposing background. (Author)

5.31　This is looking across the valley showing no.147 running towards Assegaaibos with the 04.00 train from Avontuur. The lake in the background is not a natural one, but was created for irrigation purposes. (Author)

AVONTUUR

5.32   This is the terminus of the longest two-foot gauge railway, 177 miles from Port Elizabeth and 2859ft above sea level. On 17th June 1981, NG15 no.147 is standing at the station having arrived with a goods train from Assegaaibos. 28 years after this picture was taken no.147 was preserved and put on display next to the station. (Dick Manton)

THE PATENSIE BRANCH

This branch from its junction at Gamtoos on the Avontuur line is just over seventeen miles long and was opened in 1914. Gamtoos is 23ft above sea level whilst Patensie is 180ft. In between it has 1 in 40 gradients and a highest point of 200ft at Gonnakop, two miles before Patensie. The main intermediate station on the branch is Hankey and the region is in a very fertile farming area with good water supplies from nearby rivers.

NEAR HANKEY

5.33   Coming along the valley, on 27th June 1978, with a train of empties to Patensie is this double headed train hauled by NG15 nos.133 and 146. (Author)

5.34   There are two main bridges on the branch in addition to many culverts. Here are nos.133 and 146 crossing one of the large girder bridges between Hankey and Gamtoos with a train coming down the valley on its way to Loerie on 27th June 1978. (Author)

5.35   NG15 no.148, in spotless condition, is making a run-past over the level crossing during the 'Kei Explorer Tour' organised by the Railway Society of Southern Africa on its way to Patensie on 3rd May 1989. (David C Rodgers)

5.36   The railway is now climbing through the hills to a summit near Gonnakop, before dropping down into Patensie, and this shows the two NG15s nos.133 and 146 on the hillside as they make their way to Patensie. They were photographed on 27th June 1977. (Author)

5.37   This picture from 2nd April 1986 has the fertile valley in the background and shows NG15 no.135 hauling the 10.00 goods from Patensie to Loerie near the summit of the branch. (David C Rodgers)

PATENSIE

5.38   NG15 no.135 has just arrived at the station on 2nd April 1986, with the 06.00 train from Loerie. After servicing, the engine was cleaned before its journey back to Loerie and the result is seen in the previous picture. This engine went to England and was stored on the Exmoor Steam Railway. (David C Rodgers)

5.39   A mighty effort is required by the fireman to turn no.133 on the turntable, whilst no.146 has been turned and is facing back towards Gamtoos. Both locomotives went to Wales; no.133 to the Welsh Highland Railway, no.146 to the Brecon Mountain Railway. This scene was pictured on 27th June 1978. (Author)

5.40   On the same day the photographer was pleased to find this attractive lineside location with its neat and carefully tended garden, and this shows nos.133 and 146 approaching Patensie. However, he was more than surprised on leaving the lineside to be told that he had been standing in the grounds of Patensie Open Prison, but fortunately was not taken into custody! (Author)

5.41   In the afternoon sunlight both NG15 nos.133 and 146 are working hard to get their train away from Patensie up to the line summit before their descent down towards Hankey and back to Loerie. (Author)

6. PRESERVATION

SANDSTONE
STEAM RAILROAD

This privately owned railway has built an impressive two-foot gauge line with a route mileage of just over 16 miles with its base at Hoekfontein, between Ficksburg and Fourisburg. Its nearest point of contact adjacent to Spoornet's Cape Gauge railway is at Vailima, on the Bethlehem to Bloemfontein line. By 2008 there were no less than eight SAR Garratts, in addition to many other interesting locomotives, on the railway. Two of the operational Garratts are seen below.

6.1   Double heading a charter train and passing the lake between Hoekfontein and Vailima are NGG16 class Garratts nos 153 and 113 on 12th May 2008. (Terence M Bagworth)

➜ 6.2   The same pair of Garratts are bringing their mixed train past a background of cliffs on their way back to Hoekfontein on 12th May 2008. (Terence M Bagworth)

PATON'S COUNTRY NARROW GAUGE RAILWAY

This railway uses part of the former Ixopo to Madonela branch between Allwoodburn, Ixopo, to Ncula a distance of nine miles. They own two Garratts, NGG11 no.55, in working order and NGG16 no.116, awaiting overhaul and return to service

6.3   The veteran NGG11 class Garratt no. 55, built by Beyer Peacock in 1925, is a wonderful attraction on this railway and here, on 16th May 2008, it is seen with its train near Carisbrook en route to Ncalu. The Garratt only works tourist trains if there are more than 40 passengers booked, otherwise a smaller former sugar plantation locomotive is used. (Terence M Bagworth)

WELSH HIGHLAND RAILWAY

The original railway was called the North Wales Narrow Gauge Railway and ran from Dinas to South Snowdon (Rhyd Ddu) from 1877, changed its name to the Welsh Highland Railway in 1922 and a year later extended to Portmadoc. This was short lived and all trains had ceased running by 1937. During World War 2 the line was dismantled and that seemed to be the end of the story. However, in the last years of the 20th century a remarkable resurgence was taking place to completely rebuild the entire railway and extend it northwards from its old terminus at Dinas, for just under three miles to Caernarvon. The length of line from Caernarvon to Porthmadog is 25 miles and the track was completed in 2009.

The South African engines on their roster comprise two NG15 2-8-2s nos.133 and 134 and four NGG16 Garratts nos. 87, 138, 140 and 143. The Garratts provide the main motive power on the railway and are ideally suited for hauling trains over the steep gradients and sharp curvature of the track.

6.4   Photographed on 13th October 1997, NGG 16 no.138 is seen on the historic day when the Welsh Highland Railway was opened from Caernarvon to Dinas, running round its official opening day train at Caernarvon. In the background is the impressive castle built in the 13th century by King Edward I and the birthplace of Edward II, the first Prince of Wales. (Peter Johnson)

6.5   Near Rhyd Ddu, towards the line summit, there is a splendid location and views where the train comes around reverse curves and here, on 18th September 2005, looking west towards Mynydd Mawr, green painted NGG16 class Garratt no.138, now named *Millenium*, is seen starting its journey back to Caernarvon during a Gala Event. (Author)

6.6   Looking the other way on the same day, Garratt no.143 is bringing a train from Caernarvon on the approach to Rhyd Ddu during the Gala weekend. This engine was the last steam locomotive built at Beyer Peacock's Gorton Foundry in 1958. It was one of seven Garratts ordered by the Tsumeb Corporation in South West Africa, but actually delivered to South African Railways following the decision of the Corporation to convert its railway to 3ft 6ins gauge. (Author)

WELSH HIGHLAND HERITAGE RAILWAY

6.7   Seen on 7th April 1996, stored awaiting restoration is NG15 2-8-2 no.120 at Gelert's Farm, Porthmadog. It is standing alongside operational 0-4-2T *Gelert*, built by Bagnall in 1953, two years after no.120. No.120 was sold in 2009. (Peter Johnson)

FFESTINIOG RAILWAY

6.8   Photographed on 2nd May 1997, we feast our eyes on the lovely sight of two gleaming NGG16 Garratts nos.138 (green and in steam) and 140 (maroon) at Glan y Pwll after restoration for the Welsh Highland Railway. They are being prepared for display at a gala event on the Ffestiniog Railway the next day. (Peter Johnson)

➔ 6.9 The Ffestiniog Railway also overhauled NGG16 no.87, which is seen in workshop grey livery on the Cob, near Porthmadog Harbour station, during the first day of testing after completion of its £500,000 restoration on 23rd January 2009. (Peter Johnson)

➔   6.10 Seen from the top of Ynys Tywyn, Garratt No. 87 steams away from Harbour station and onto Britannia Bridge at 07.20 on Monday, 23rd March 2009, thus becoming the first steam locomotive to run from Porthmadog to Dinas since the closure of the WHR in 1937. An opening date for passenger traffic over the bridge was awaited. FR traffic ran across the bridge from 1836. (Roger Dimmick)

Middleton Press

EVOLVING THE ULTIMATE RAIL ENCYCLOPEDIA

Easebourne Lane, Midhurst, West Sussex.
GU29 9AZ   Tel:01730 813169
www.middletonpress.co.uk   email:info@middletonpress.co.uk
A-978 0 906520   B- 978 1 873793   C- 978 1 901706   D-978 1 904474
E - 978 1 906008   F - 978 1 908174

All titles listed below were in print at time of publication - please check current availability by looking at our website - *www.middletonpress.co.uk* or by requesting a Brochure which includes our *LATEST* RAILWAY TITLES also our TRAMWAY, TROLLEYBUS, MILITARY and COASTAL series